MEMORIES OF OLD POPLAR

by John Blake

STEPNEY BOOKS PUBLICATIONS

Acknowledgements

Thanks to the Tower Hamlets Local History Library, Bancroft Road, E1 for photographs from the Whiffen Collection and Tower Hamlets Planning Department for the use of photographs.

ISBN 0 9505241 1 5

First published by Stepney Books Publications, 1977
c/o 19 Tomlins Grove, Bow, London E3 4NX

Reprinted August 1982

2nd edition, 1995

Printed by Aldgate Press
3 Gunthorpe Street, E1

FOREWORD

Foreword

Whilst sitting at home and talking together with the family and old friends, I thought it would be a good idea, if I could cast my mind back to some of the old days spent at Poplar in the Dock area. Hence, I decided to try to write of some memories of days gone by. Having lived for many years in the area around St Michaels Church, I have endeavoured to portray events and family life throughout the era, from Edwardian times. Vast changes have taken place, in the environment of Poplar, and for the older people, only memories of the past Poplar hectic life remain, and I have tried to depict these happenings. I may have digressed at times, but I have tried to give a picture of everyday life as I saw it, taking place during the years my family and I lived in Poplar.

When I had completed the task, I sought the advice of Mr Bernard Nurse, Local Historian, at the Central Library, Bancroft Road, London, E1. I am very grateful for the encouragement he gave me, and I am pleased to make this acknowledgement to him, as I am sure, if he had given me an adverse reply, I probably would not have troubled to write at all.

John Blake 1972

Note to the Second Edition

When this edition was being prepared for printing, John Blake's original hand-drawn map of Poplar streets and shops came to light. It has been re-drawn for publication by Donald Mullis.

The photograph of Poplar Station on page 41 replaces a picture of Millwall Junction, now untraceable.

1.

St Michael and All Angels Church

St Michael and All Angels Church has always played a tremendous part in the life of Poplar, especially in the square mile that surrounded it. The lighted clock was a beacon, seen by all around, and every household checked their time by it. It bore a great history of spreading the gospel, and its social activities were important throughout the area. I was married there, and so were most of my relatives. I can remember it from my early childhood days, and some of the clergy who delivered sermons from within and without the Church. I can remember the Reverends Preston, Marshall, Phillimore, Langdon, Ashcroft and Tuck, also the venerable brothers Groser, known to all and sundry as Father John and Jack. The two brothers made a great impact on all the people, and became known to everyone. They had short hair and wore a long gown, similar to a monk, and a crucifix hung on their chest. They mixed in with all the people, and even went into the pub for a drink and a chat. One of the brothers was a member of the Poplar Council, and they both mixed in with the workers, and tried to share their troubles, wherever they found it needed. I remember, an incident during the 1926 general strike, when a meeting was being held, in the original Poplar Town Hall, in Newby Place. It was being addressed by Emanuel Shinwell, and the hall was packed to its fullest capacity, consequently the crowd began to accumulate outside, in the road, not being able to obtain admittance. Among them, I could see the figure of Father John, trying to keep them quiet and orderly, but the security forces were soon on the scene, clearing the crowds away, including the Reverend gentleman who was striving to appeal for tolerance on both sides. They were split up eventually, one, Father John, going to a new living in Cable Street, the other brother, Father Jack, went to a hamlet in Cornwall.

I wonder how many baptisms were carried out at the font, just inside the Church doors. They built a 'stable' to the left of the altar, to celebrate the festival of Christmas, which was viewed by the congregation. There was an occasion when police officers performed the duties of Sidesmen in the Church. There were occasions also when the Church brass band toured the streets and held outdoor services with other churches from the locality. There were social schemes and fellowship clubs, bazaars, jumble sales and all

St Michael and All Angels Church with War Memorial in front
(LBTH Planning Dept.)

manner of activities. There was a 'Harmonic' Society, and under that banner a new hall was erected, next door to the Church, in Ullin Street which is still standing. Downstairs were various small rooms, and a large hall upstairs contained a small stage, fully furnished. Meetings and concerts were held here, and Saturday night was a feature 'Harmonic' night, with variety shows, and I remember that a chairman sat at a table in front of the stage, announcing the different acts that were to appear. To the right of the stage was a refreshment bar. The cup of coffee and slice of fruit cake were in great demand. For the lovers of boxing, they ran shows of the 'noble art' there. It was a custom of the time that most parents made sure that the children attended Sunday School on Sunday afternoons, and many of them were in the Church choir.

The vicarage windows were behind the War Memorial, facing St Leonards Road, and an author who used the name of Eileen Baillie, but who was actually a daughter of the vicar of St Michael's Church at the time, used to sit at the windows, observing the everyday life of the local people. She produced at least one book about Poplar, 'Shabby Paradise' which is available at all the local libraries. In front of those windows, in the road outside, and facing the roads and streets adjacent to the Church, stands the War Memorial, upon which are inscribed the names of many past inhabitants of Poplar and Bromley by Bow, who gave their lives in the fight for survival in two World Wars. Large numbers of them were members of the congregation, and were baptised there, or were married at its altar. There used to be packed congregations, and many workers for the Church. Many of those whose names are recorded on the Memorial went there. I can remember how great a part religion played in the lives of the Poplar people years ago, and there was a wide variety of places of worship as well as outdoor services in the streets. I remember All Hallows, St Saviours, St Stephens, Trinity Church, Wesleyan, St Frideswides, the Salvation Army, Poplar and Bromley Tabernacle, Bromley St Leonards, the Catholic Church in Canton Street and Poplar church. There were also small mission halls of every denomination.

2.

Family Life

My mother and father lived at 105 Teviot Street, Poplar, and I was born there in 1899. They afterwards moved to the next turning, Spey Street, and from there to 6 Andrew Street, Poplar, where we lived for many years. When I reached the age of 21 I got married and went to live with my wife at 85 Willis Street, Poplar. These streets are all adjacent to St Leonards Road, Poplar, and near St Michael's Church. I had three brothers and three sisters. I was the eldest, and the others were born at various intervals throughout the years that followed. My father worked for many years, as a plumber's mate, in the ship-repairing firm of R.H. Green and Silley Weir, at their Blackwall yard. He had to work for long hours and the wages were small, but it was a living, and it was the mainstay to pay rent, clothe and feed seven youngsters, besides all other household expenses, such as food and clothes for himself and his wife. His main amusement, in return, was a drink at the local with his mates at the weekend. Most of the families living in Poplar were of the same dimensions, and their world revolved around similar concerns of family and budget. The main saviour of the household was the most important person, our Mother. The same applies in every family, and even in these modern times, everyone has to rely on her just as they did in Edwardian times. When any of the children had any problem or worry of any description on their mind, they only had to unfold their mind to Mum, who immediately soothed their fears. Like the majority of the neighbours, she had to augment her income from the weekly wage packet from Dad, by full use of the tallyman and the pawnbroker. All this was necessary to bring up a family and meet household expenses in a decent way. True, Dad had to work hard for the cash necessary to run the household, but, naturally, when he handed over his quota to Mum, and he had kept a small amount for pocket money, he considered his duty had been carried out, but Mum only started from then, with all the worry of making ends meet. Seven of us children required constant renewals of footwear and clothing and that went on until we were all old enough to go to work and earn a few bob. That meant running up bills on the 'never-never' with the tallymen, who took weekly payments off the main debt, plus interest. At times, I expect, we all had to go to the door, when the tallyman knocked for his weekly payment, and say, 'Please Mum says she's out, could you please leave it till next week?'

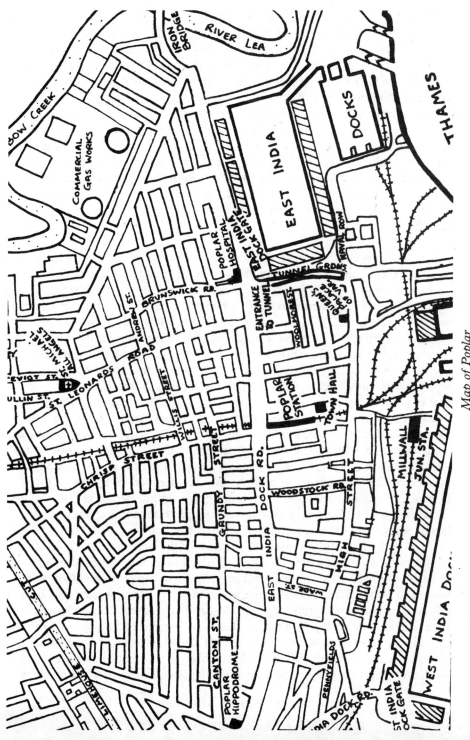

Map of Poplar

Women used to sell second hand clothing in the gutter outside the 'Young Prince' pub in Chrisp Street, Poplar, and Mum had to go there and try to obtain a bargain in second hand boots or clothing. During the early years, from 1900 onwards to the first World War, all these things were part of the everyday life in the East End of London. Sometimes one of us would get the job from Mum to go next door and borrow a penny for the gas. When we had got it, the operation followed of climbing on the stair banisters to reach the gas meter, which was on a shelf over a door in the passage, and then inserting the copper coin. The gas mantle was a flimsy affair, and only gave a small light, anyway, that's all we had, as electricity was not available for the masses at that time. Mum had her mother living in an upstairs room, and all she had was an oil lamp on the table for light, she had to do any reading with the air of a cheap pair of plain rimmed glasses which she had bought for herself.

The little kitchen where we all congregated was very cosy. It contained a food cupboard and dresser for the china, over the mantelpiece was an overmantel, and a mantel border hung right around the front of the mantelpiece. Usually there was a string hanging from end to end, for drying purposes. There were plenty of vases etc, also on view. Below was the fireplace, in front of which was a fireguard of wire meshing. In the winter months there was always a fire, which not only heated the kitchen, but the oven also. A kettle was always at the ready on top of the stove. A door separated the little kitchen from the passage leading to the street door. The coal or coke was kept in a cupboard in the passage. The coal was brought off a coalman, delivering round the district, and the coke we got from the gasworks in Levens Road, Poplar, in an old pram, or handcart, which we had made ourselves. Mum used to go to Coppens in Chrisp Street, for buying the 'Ostend Rabbit', all cleaned and skinned, or take a jug for some eels and mashed, which were cut up in portions in your presence, or by way of a change, pie and mashed covered with hot gravy. Mum used to get two penny-worth of bacon bones, which was enough to fill a saucepan, or make faggot stews, with onions, turnips, and carrots and stewing meat, this was cooked on the stove simmering over the heat of the fire, and the whole of the family made short work of such a feast. To add to all this, we children used to dash out of school at midday, and make haste to the Jerusalem Coffee Rooms in Follett Street, for a dinner say of meat pie, potatoes and cabbage, followed by plain and syrup, or plum duff, and cup of tea. These dinners were provided every day, and my brothers and sisters and I enjoyed them very much. The tickets were provided to all school children at London County Council Schools. Mum would often get a half pint of porter at the local, and when she got it home, she put the poker into the fire and made it red hot. She then inserted it into the jug of porter. She then took it up to her mother in the upstairs front room. This was a custom at that time, amongst all the people. She got one of the children to go to Mrs Wham, who had a general shop at the bottom of Andrew Street. A cup was handed over for ½d of jam, ½d pickles, 1d cheese, a lump of salt, ¼ or ½lb of margarine, ½lb sugar, loose, weighed and done up in a paper bag. Around this time the grown ups could purchase a packet of Weights for 2d, Woodbines, Park Drive or Bandmaster were the same price – ½oz Nut Brown and packet of A.G. cigarette papers was 4d. The dearer cigarettes were Players 'Medium', Gold Flakes, Capstans – Lloyds Scented – all these at double that price. The cigarettes were in packets of ten, but they could be bought in fives.

Mother had another important job on Saturdays, as she had to redeem Dad's suit from the pawnshop, so that he could wear it over the weekend. He had to keep up appearances when he visited the pub for the weekend session with his mates. He had strict instructions from Mum not to spill any beer on it, because if he did so, she would not be able to get the same price on it from the pawnbroker on the Monday morning. And when she took it, there was a charge of 2d for brown paper, 1d for the loan of a hanger. I was always interested in the ticket machine on the counter of a pawnbroker. The shop assistant operated three pens at once and the tickets were completed in one motion. The three pens all worked in unison and three tickets were filled in automatically. The first one went to the customer, one on the package pawned, and one was filed by the pawnbroker for record. Another useful apparatus was in use by Oxenhams, Drapers, in Chrisp Street, Poplar. An overhead rail ran the length of the shop over the counter. It had connections with a cashier's office, at the far end. When the customer had made a purchase, the shop assistant put the bill and cash in a small ball, which she hoisted to the rail above, and it was propelled along the rail to the cashier, who receipted the bill and placed any change in the ball, which was returned along the rail to the counter, where the customer was waiting, and the transaction was completed by handing over the bill and change.

The Childrens Country Holiday Fund was used to provide a holiday once a year for schoolchildren in Poplar and other places. They were gathered together and formed into a party, and taken by rail from London to various country areas, and billeted there with local people. We all went and had a very enjoyable time. The Ragged School Union also used to give the very poor children outings, and on these occasions each child had to have a label attached to a string around their neck, to identify them. Mum was often questioned by the children as to whether she wanted any bread fetching; of course she never asked why they were so anxious to get it because she knew that with every loaf of bread bought from one of the local bakers shops, there was a big hunk of free mince pice, covered with sugar handed over. Beautiful crusty cottage loaves were baked on the premises by most bakers. Our Mum, like all other mothers, had plenty to occupy her mind, doing the daily chores; the foot-scraper outside the front door had to be polished with blacklead, and the knocker on the door, the step and window ledge had to be scrubbed, and indoors the fireplace had to be cleaned out and all the ashes removed and the fire relaid, do the sweeping up, make beds, and washing up. Then out in the yard, in fair weather or foul, scrubbing at the galvanised bath, turning the heavy wringer and hanging the washing on the line. Later it all had to be ironed, between getting some shopping and preparing meals. How it was all done by one pair of hands goodness knows. In the days before the First War, street doors of every house were always open, and were not shut till bed-time at night. Anyone feeling lonely only had to stand at the door, and in a short time someone would come along and have a chat and cheer their neighbour up.

At Christmas time, in the era of our childhood days, it was the custom to hang up the stocking at the end of the bed for filling with Christmas gifts. Mum used to gather up little items as time went on, and some sweets and fruit and nuts, and wrap them up in fancy paper. She and Dad used to save up little odd amounts of money to provide these gifts. Of course, times have changed, and children of today would not think much of this, but the children of that day thought more of these little items than they do today. Parents of today are able to give their children more expensive gifts than was possible years ago. Mum made up some paper chains, with a festive bell hanging in the middle, and had them stretched across the top of the room from wall to wall. Dad would get a few crates of beer in, which he paid for in a Christmas Club, and if possible, a rabbit and chicken to enlarge the Christmas dinner for themselves and seven children, followed of course by the Christmas pudding, which had been made a couple of weeks before. The shopkeepers and landlords of the locals used to give a gift to all the regular customers who had dealt with them all the year round. The shop windows were all illuminated with fairy lights and displays of holly, mistletoe, tinsel, and the same applied to all the stalls in Chrisp Street, Poplar. Even if there was snow and cold, the churches would send round their choirs to sing carols. After the Christmas morning excitement of unpacking the stockings, the whole of the family got ready to gather round the kitchen table and make inroads into the dinner. Friends or relatives would call round, and the day would finish with a sing song in the front room. Mum would then probably sit back and feel contented that she had carried out her duties to the family for Yuletide.

There was a piano in the front room of our house, and when Mum got the time, she would like to play it. Years before she got married, she used to teach the pupils the art of piano playing, and so the keyboard did not come strange to her. She could play from music or by ear. Her chance came when Dad had been quenching his thirst at the local with his mates, and came home a little on the merry side. He would regale us all with tales of the past, and about his ancestors, and we would all sit round him in the little kitchen till he had unfolded all he could think of. He suddenly decided he would give us a rendering of his 'Song and Dance Act'. Mum was recruited to provide the background music on the piano. He commenced in the front room with a favourite ditty which had unending verses. The opening bars were 'A Fortnight Ago Boys', chorus after chorus rang out, and when they had finally finished he began his step dance. True, he was no G.H. Elliott, but his performances were always better when he had supped an ale or two. It's a wonderful thing what a few 2d pints of beer would do, anyway, these things I have mentioned were enjoyed by all of us in the family. After all, money was short, and we, like many other families, made the most of whatever we had and took things as they came. We were lucky, as we all went to school reasonably dressed and nourished, and all enjoyed pretty good health, which was something to be grateful for. Some children who went to school in those early days never had any shoes and stockings, and went barefoot. They were 'elementary' schools, but we received lessons in reading, writing and arithmetic, besides other subjects, which stood us in great stead later.

Mum and Dad used to like a little gamble, which was likely to make the bookie tremble in his shoes. These punters had no fear, they would lay out sixpence each way, without turning a hair. Dad would tell Mum, that he had 'sorted out a horse', after intense perusal of the 'Midday Star'. He had weighed the past form of the horse, the thorough preparation of the training and the fact that a top jockey had the mount. He had a summit meeting with his partner, and after lengthy discussion they arrived at a decision as to the horse they were going to squander their great wager on. Mum got a little nervous and asked Dad if he thought they had done a wise deed. He calmed her fears and said if ever there was a racing cert, this was it, and so the wager was laid; sixpence win and sixpence place. The sound of the paper boy later was heard outside the front door, and one of us was sent to get the 'Star'. Dad looked at the Racing Results and became very quiet. Mum looked across to him. She did not like the look of things, and eventually Dad told her that his cert had got third. She asked Dad 'How much place money do we get?' He acquainted her with the news that there were only three runners. Third in a field of three. What a triumph! It was some time before Dad lived that one down. Anyway, it gave them happiness to have a little flutter now and again.

Any household illness had to be cured by old fashioned remedies, as a doctor's fee could not always be afforded. Epsom Salts, Brimstone and Treacle, Carbonate of Soda, Camphorated Oil and Amber, Russian Tallow and Brown Paper, Vinegar and Brown Paper for a headache, Baked Salt on a flannel applied to face for toothache, Bread Poultice applied to any septic condition, children with cuts or bruises were taken to nurses in Bow Lane. Another remedy used in those early days was hot fomentations of lint and iodine, applied to the skin for rheumatic or similar complaints. It was said that alcohol and meat was a prime cause of contracting these rheumatic ailments, due to the forming of uric acid. The working class, after their labours, were glad to partake of a pint or two, and thus in those days bouts of gout were very prevalent. This was a very painful affliction, and was so tender that the sufferer could not even bear anyone walking by it without flinching.

There is a story attached to this, which may bear repeating. It was a very cold winter, and our father suddenly became a victim of the gout. He naturally had to lay up from work, and Mum had to gather up all the items necessary for the treatment of this painful ailment. He didn't want to take to bed, and she made up a nice fire and pillowed up his armchair, standing it near the fireplace. The little kitchen soon got very warm, and Dad composed himself in the armchair and waited for Mum to administer the laying on of the red-hot poultice to the inflamed ankle joint. Mum fixed his leg up on a stool in front of him, and she told Dad to brace himself. She held the hot lint at the end of a wooden spoon and began the count down, and when she reached zero she smacked it down on the painful ankle. Dad acted very bravely under the operation, and did not flinch or utter a sound. Mum wrapped cotton wool and bandage all round the lint and fixed a covering over the padding. Dad got out his packet of Nut Brown tobacco and packet of AG cigarette papers and made a few fags up. Mum made the fire up and said to Dad: 'I must go out to get some errands, so keep yourself warm. There are no callers to come, so you've got nothing to worry about till I get back. Don't knock your ankle.' Dad said to Mum, as she prepared to go out, 'Keep well wrapped up, and get back as soon as you can, as it's very cold outside.' He sat back in the chair, and relaxed in the warm air of the kitchen, and was on the point of dozing off when there was a loud knock at the front door. He mused to himself, it couldn't be anyone important, as she said before she went out, that no callers were expected, so he decided to take no action. However there was another loud knock at the front door, which he again ignored. A third time came a very much louder knock, and suddenly the thought struck him, that Mum had perhaps forgotten to take her street door key, and was standing outside, in the bitter cold wind. Dad made a quick decision, to act immediately, and so, with great fortitude, he removed the 'scaffolding' all around the inflamed joint, and gingerly lifted his foot off the stool, onto the kitchen floor. He managed to get across the kitchen, and open the passage door, and then he had to mount two steps which led to the passage and as this was very long, he had to grip hold of the banisters. As he struggled along towards the door, the knocker of which was still being banged, he shouted out, 'I'll get there as soon as I can,' as it was a great effort to get there at all. He gradually got to the door, paused to get his breath, and eventually opened it. It was not mum, but a canvasser, who inquired, 'Do you want to buy the famous Old Moore's Almanac?' Dad was a fairly good-tempered man, but I am afraid, if you searched the works of Shakespeare, you would not find any mention of the sort of reply that the gout-ridden sufferer gave to the caller. He slammed the door and fought his way back down the long passage to the comfort and warmth of the kitchen, managed to sit down and get his foot up again on the stool, fixing all the 'scaffolding' round as best he could.

My sisters went their way for games, and my brothers and I went ours. Once a week, as soon as I left Culloden Street School, I would go across road to the shop and get my copy of the 'Magnet', which contained the adventures of Harry Wharton, Bob Cherry, Inky, Loder, Mr Quelch, Mr Locke, and among others Billy Bunter (The Owl). All the tales and scenes centred around Greyfriars School. There were rivals in the 'Gem', and the comic 'Chips', and all these periodicals were in great demand by the schoolboys of that age. After our evening meal, Mum used to lose us, and we would get out with our mates. We used to run races from the bottom of Andrew Street, in Brunswick Road, as far as the Poplar and Bromley Tabernacle; and at different times we were busy with Yo Yo, spinning peg tops, diabolo, and playing for picture cards, which were in every packet of cigarettes – the idea was to blow over for a win. The girls had their pursuits, such as tying a rope on a lamp-post and swinging round on it, Hop Scotch, Skipping, Maypole, Bonce and Gobs. Of course, football and cricket were top of the charts.

When Easter tide came round we used to help Dad do the regular job which had to be done every year at this time. It was white-washing all the back yard walls and all the back of the house was thoroughly done. The spring cleaning had to include an examination of the walls inside the house, in case of the arrival of any bugs. A room might have to be decorated, and that meant whitewashing the ceiling, repapering walls, and painting doors. All the family 'mucked in', and someone was detailed to go to Haines Fish Shop in St Leonards Road for ha'penny bit and

Marbles

Swinging

(from 'Living London'
George R. Sims)

Rounders

Hopscotch

Tops

ha'porth of chips for each member of the family. If there were any available, a bag full of cracklings was bought for a few coppers.

Fashions and habits all change as time goes on, and we children were all growing up and going out to work and entering into new paths of life. The home family was being left behind, as we all got married and left to make homes of our own. The system of marriage in those days was a Church ceremony, with a choir, and the church bells ringing. When the service had been completed, the bride and groom and all the wedding guests celebrated the occasion. Of course, in this day and age, the bride's parents have to foot the bill for a big reception in a hall with catering, drinks and music laid on, according to etiquette. Years ago young ladies were expected to be home by ten thirty any night they had been out with their chap, and to stay out overnight was considered strictly unthinkable, and it was not allowed to go on. They were not allowed to go away for holiday without permission, which was rarely given, and to walk along the street smoking would brand them 'fast'.

The little kitchen, which contained Mum and Dad and seven children, was being gradually cleared of its occupants. We all had our different occupations, and entered into a new life with our marriage partners, and moved on to different accommodation, hoping to rear our own families, and try to bring them up with the same love and care that we had always received from our Mum and Dad, after their many years of struggling to give us a decent chance in life, which required self-denial, devotion and constant effort on their part. They never knew what it was like to have a week's holiday anywhere, and they had very few days out either. Like most of the parents of those years, they gave up everything for us.

Cherry-Bobs

3.

Outdoor Life

East India Docks was a hive of industry, load after load of merchandise going in and out of the docks, forwarding to, and collecting from, all corners of the earth. Ships of many lines, such as Union Castle, and Elder & Fyffes, used the dock regularly, as did many others. Opposite, in East India Dock Road, was the Poplar Hospital for Accidents, where sterling work was done throughout the years, dealing with accidents which happened throughout the area. Bernard Baron donated and built an annexe to the hospital. Some of the wards were named after benefactors, who had helped the upkeep of the hospital. One special night in my memory was the night of the Silvertown explosion, at a chemical works. There were many injured, and those unfortunate people were brought by any means available, to Poplar Hospital. Doctor Bray, who was the house surgeon at the time, was dealing with the patients out in the road, and detailing some inside, and others to the London and various hospitals all round. He was a great lover of the Boxing Art, and used to be a regular visitor to the National Sporting Club. He afterwards continued his good work at St Andrews Hospital. He was originally a general practitioner who worked from a surgery in Montague Place, off Bow Lane Poplar, and when he branched into other fields, he was followed by a Doctor Hayden Jones who used to ride around the Borough in plus fours, on a cycle, and he had a cheery smile for everyone he passed on his journeys, both old and young. Doctor Jones, it was said, was a Welsh rugby player in his student days. Poplar also had the services of Doctor Dunlop, who came from Scotland, and called every woman who called on him 'lass'. The immaculately dressed Dr Spillane, whose surgery was in St Leonards Road, always looked the acme of fashion and as he strolled along he was attired in frock coat, striped trousers, with spats over his shoes, starched white collar and tie, and top hat, umbrella on his arm, and valise in his hand. He never passed anyone without a nod. I recall Dr Jessiman and Dr Hendry, and, of course, there were many others that I never had occasion to meet. We all used to belong to the 'Hospital Savings Assn.', who provided funds, also the Hospital Saturday Fund, who gave great help.

In the early days of the century, when the air was laden with factory and locomotive smoke, which caused frequent fogs, the main street lighting was by gas light. A regular sight was to see the attendant walking through the thoroughfares, carrying a pole on his shoulder, long enough to reach the gas lamp, at the top of the lamp post. He made his rounds at dusk, putting on the light with the pole, and at dawn putting it out by the same method. The road traffic consisted of Hansom cabs, carriages, coaches, horse buses and trams, brakes, fire engines, water carts, delivery vans and all vehicles that were drawn by the horse. Many used to use the cycle to get to and from work, and for pleasure jaunts. The policemen, who were proceeding to their beat on the streets, came from Poplar Police Station, in East India Dock Road. A sergeant in charge walked with them to each 'detail'. A familiar sight was the handcart, with two policemen in attendance, upon which was a drunk. The handcart was wheeled into the back entrance of the station. Many people, in bed at nights, got a comforting thought when they heard the sound of the policeman's boots as he walked on his rounds during the night. The road workers, repairing roads wore 'knee irons' as a form of protection against dirt or rodents. These were straps placed just below the knee. A night watchman had to take charge at the end of the day's work, and first job was to light all the red lamps and hang them round the guard ropes on the site. He would then light a big coke fire and sit in the hut provided, usually smoking a broken clay pipe. Other frequent sights were the chimney sweep with tubes and brushes slung over his back, the postman delivering and collecting the mail, wearing a frock coat type of brass buttoned uniform and a double peaked hat. The rag man with his barrow, shouting 'Any rags bottles or bones' even 'rabbit skins'. The hokey pokey man with his small cart furnished with a tub containing ice cream, which he dug out for wafers and cornets with a wooden spoon. His shout was 'Hokey Pokey Penny a Lump'. The window repairer with his 'rack', containing glass, on his back. The vendor with baskets on a barrow, containing mussels, fine large shrimps, winkles and cockles. As he went along, he shouted 'Fine large shrimps'. The muffin man, with handbell in his hand, and tray of muffins on his head. The milkman with his striped apron and straw hat, selling milk from his barrow by scooping it into the housewife's jug. Stewart's Dairy, in Grundy Street, used to have a cow led through the streets. Some of the shops at Christmas time used to have a cow on view to the public, usually in a disused stable adjacent to Chrisp Street Market.

Chrisp Street Market was always a lively place, and I can recall all sorts of diversions there. There was a group of girls, who, after laying crossed swords on the ground, executed a Scottish Sword Dance, to the sound of the bagpipes. There was often a group who spread some boards in the gutter, and gave a 'drag' act, singing and dancing to the tune of the barrel organ. The Pearly Kings and Queens toured the Borough, gathering in cash for

Coalman

Baked Potatoes

Baked Chestnuts

Taking a sample of milk

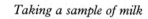

(from 'Living London'
George R. Sims)

deserving causes. The Salvation Army lasses visited the pubs and other places with copies of 'War Cry'. This religious body has done great work for 'Down and Outs'. The doors of their homes are never shut, and bed and breakfast are never refused. There was the man selling hot baked potatoes or hot chestnuts or sarsaparilla from a barrow. A male and female singer advertising and selling sheet music, which was posted all over the back of a barrel organ which furnished the necessary background melody. The foreign seamen when on leave after a voyage, used to walk about the streets in 'Indian File', one behind the other, and they often used to make their way to Chrisp Street and go to the second hand clothing stores, or stalls. The 'boys' operating the sale manipulated the prices so that the customers went away happy and satisfied. There was the vendor who in a loud voice extolled the virtues of his cough mixture. Previously he had been speaking with effort and a hoarse voice, and to impress the audience he had sipped a drop of the mixture, to prove he had gained an instant cure. The vendor operating the sale of teasets and dinner services, the patter and repartee of the salesmen helped the trade along. One thing especially exciting to us children was the sight of a fire engine, called out to a fire, drawn by galloping horses, as it sped along to the clanging of a bell being rung by one of the brass-helmeted firemen, standing on one of the steps that surrounded the fire engine.

A big event in Poplar was always the annual Catholic Parade. Many houses in High Street, Wade Street and all round used to take out the windows adjacent to the street, and instal an altar. When the procession started from Canton Street, it was composed mainly of little children, all dressed in beautiful clothes, which must have cost a great deal of money, and immense hard work by the parents. Bands were marching in front of the procession, and everyone in the district used to line up and watch it pass, then later walk round the streets, admiring the altars and decorations. King George V and Queen Mary toured all round the streets one Sunday afternoon, and spoke to people at various places in the Borough, and another time there was a visit by Gandhi, who was greatly impressed.

East India Dock Road, from the tunnel to Burdett Road, was the gathering place of thousands of people on Saturday or Sunday evening. There were so many people congregated there on the 'Weekend Walk', that, in order to avoid accidents, where they had to walk into the road to get by, the Borough Council had guard rails erected along the road. All the teenagers walked up and down here, and it was known as 'Monkey's Parade'. More romances went on here than in any other part of Poplar, I think. The lads used to wear the latest fashions of the day, as did the girls. In between the two world wars, the lads wore an outfit such as this: 'Bulldog' toe boots,

Horse-drawn Fire Engine (from 'Living London' George R. Sims)

Catholic Procession in Rook Street, Poplar 1926
(Local History Library, Tower Hamlets Libraries)

block-shoulder jackets, a waistcoat, cut low at front, pleated front silk shirt, a blue bow with white spots, attached to a stud at the back of bow, 'peg top' trousers, wide at the top, tapering down to narrow bottoms. The cap was worn at a jaunty angle, there was half a cane in front of the cap and leaving two dents in the back. The girls had their idea of fashion also, and whatever the latest fashion was in vogue at the time either sex took advantage of it, small hats or large hats, low or high heeled shoes, hobble skirts, short or long dresses and skirts, woollen muffs, open at both ends, so that the hands could be inserted for warmth in wintry conditions. The boys had all different types of footwear, headgear, trousers, shirts, caps, in fact anything that was worn to be up to date with the trend of the time.

One of the sights I can remember in the twenties was the paper boys who collected their quires of newspapers at Raggetts or Rubys in St Leonards Road, the newsagents who served the area. Some of them had very poor boots on their feet, but that didn't hinder them, as they raced at top speed, through the streets, shouting 'Star', 'News', or 'Standard'. All the Winners or Football results. When the Annual Boat Race between crews from Cambridge and Oxford was being rowed on the Thames, the evening paper was printed in the colour of the winning crew light blue or dark blue. Cambridge wore light blue and Oxford dark blue. The paper boys were experts, and as soon as they spotted the customer, they knew what paper he wanted, and slipped the right copy out from the sheaf of papers under their arm, collected the proffered coin, in one motion, and sped on. As soon as they had sold out, they ran back to the newsagent for more copies. The Barber's shop, years ago, in the 'short back and sides' days was a hotbed of discussion among the customers, and while they were waiting their time to be ushered into the chair, for shaving or haircut, every subject under the sun was debated, such as politics, football, weather conditions, horses, work problems, boxing, the opposite sex, in fact nothing was left. The barber, for the purpose of diplomacy, had to make sure he didn't lean more to the one side of the argument than the other. He had to opinionate himself to the old adage that each customer was right, even if he thought him wrong. To speed up the service, lather boys were employed, and while the barber was shaving one customer, the next customer was being lathered by the boy, so he was able to shave right away. Some customers had their own shaving mugs, and these were on rack all ready, and for their private use only. Most barbers used to stock a toy, such as a wooden monkey up a stick. These were used for first haircut boys, usually brought to the barber by the father or mother of the offspring. This was very often a screaming session, as the barber assumed the proportions of a Dracula. A board was placed across the barber's chair, over the arms, for the child to sit on. The father or mother had to keep on handing out threats or 'kid stakes', and the barber tried handing over the wooden toy before he wielded the scissors, very often he had to take evasive action or risk becoming a target for the wooden toy aimed at his head. When eventually the operation had been completed, and the kid pacified, everyone sighed at a job well done. After that experience, there was not much trouble on future occasions.

In later years of our family life, when we were married, a favourite family trip on Saturday evenings, after getting dressed up, was walking past all the lighted shops in St Leonards Road, past the Gin Palace, which had a long corridor, leading to the various bars, which was ideal, if children had been taken also, and parents used to get the children a ha'penny bit of fish and ha'porth of chips, or an orange, apple, or nuts, and that gave the parents a chance to slip in the bar for a drink, whilst the children were enjoying themselves in the corridor. Then the family moved on, to walk up the East India Dock Road to Chrisp Street, which was only narrow. The pavements, and middle of the street, were packed with people. Shops were all lit up, and stalls were illuminated by flares. Woolworths 3d and 6d store was crowded. Nothing over these old currency prices were charged. The Guy Earl of Warwick pub was similar to the Gin Palace, with the same facilities for kids. After viewing all the stalls and shops time had passed sufficiently for the family to make their way home. At night, there were many coffee stalls in operation, and steaming hot cups of tea or coffee – hot saveloy and bread-cheesecakes were on sale. Horse drawn van loads of hay used to travel up East India Dock Road on the way from Essex farms to the haymarket, which was held in Aldgate, at the train terminus. It was discontinued in 1928, after being held for many years in the early hours of the morning. The driver of the van, containing hay, used to be perched up on the dickie of the van, with a safety chain around his waist. If he fell asleep, it did not matter, if he wanted a cup of hot coffee, as the horse, automatically pulled into the kerb, at the coffee stall. 'Good Pull up for Carmen' was the coffee shop sign, and workers were able to get good value for money, 'Cut from the Joint', Cottage and Shepherds Pie, Chop Toad, Eggs and Bacon, Dripping Toast, Plum Duff, Plain and Syrup, Fruit and Custard. All the coffee shops were a boon to workers and those who worked in the city could get similar cheap meals in Lockharts Restaurants.

The bend in the river housed Millwall, and Cubitt Town, or the Isle of Dogs. The people who lived and worked on 'the Island' never had any entertainment, only the pub, and very few shops. Years ago, there was no transport off the island, only the little railway from North Greenwich Station to Millwall Junction Poplar. It was a long walk up to Chrisp St. Market through the dock bridges, along Prestons Road, or the other way through West India Dock Road to East India Dock Road. There were a great number of firms settled there, which kept a large number of the local population in work. Of course, there was the island gardens, with its view of Greenwich, and this was a lovely view point for seeing the boat races, between rival crews, followed by small boats, and the steamer 'Ich Dien'. This was viewed also by people congregated on Blackwall Pier, reached by walking through Tunnel Gardens and Naval Row. On Sunday bands played in the Island gardens, and at Poplar, in the Recreation Ground, and Tunnel Gardens. It was a hive of industry on 'the Island', with firms such as Millwall Docks, Maconochie Bros, Mortons, Westwoods, East Ferry Road Engineering Works, John Lenanton, Lion Packing, Oil Wharves, George Clark, Lacke Lancaster, and many others. They had professional football there, years ago, when Millwall Football and Athletics Club commenced their activities at the Farm Road Club, commonly called the 'Mudshoot', though they are now at The Den, New Cross.

Further westwards was the Chinese Quarter, at Pennyfields, off High Street, and West India Dock Road. Also across the road was Charlie Brown's, a pub which contained many relics and gathered from the corners of the earth, brought there after voyages by seamen of all nationalities. The Royal National Lifeboat Institution had their premises in Orchard Place, Poplar, used for the construction and equipment of lifeboats. The 'Trinity House' had their works in Barchester Street, Poplar, and were responsible for equipment such as buoys, lighthouse stores, and machinery, and all sea warning devices necessary to the safe passage of shipping. The Board of Trade offices were in East India Dock Road, and seamen's hostels. The old East India Dock Gates and clock, and the splendid entrance to the old Blackwall Tunnel, have gone now, but it would be an imposing sight if they could be rebuilt at an open space, for viewing by generations to come. Many scenes in the past history of Poplar were enacted in front of those gates. Religion and politics were paramount, and many marches started from those entrances. Naval Row, at the back of the tunnel entrance, has many historic tales attached to it. Many have been quoted in the 'Steamship' pub.

Round about September, Poplar became the scene of great activity. Families were gathering up small items of furniture, cooking utensils and clothing, and preparing for the annual hop picking holiday in Kent. On the day of departure, lorries were calling at the door for the luggage, and the holidaymakers, after loading it up, all settled onto the lorry and were soon en route to the hopfields, singing lustily and hoping for good weather, so they could earn enough to pay for the enjoyment of this type of holiday. After work in the fields was completed, they used to gather in the local pubs adjacent to the farms, and have a sing song and dance. Many friendships were made among neighbours during this working holiday. Whole families, from the youngest child up, used to take advantage of this trip. Bank Holiday was enjoyed by many Poplar people, some families went to Blackheath Fair, Wanstead Flats, or cheap day trips by bus or train to the countryside to Hainault, Epping Forest, Abridge, and other beauty spots. Many used to line up outside Bromley by Bow Station with the family, to get a day return ticket on the London, Tilbury and Southend line, at the price of half a crown. When the train for Southend came to the station, it was already packed, every seat taken on its journey from Fenchurch Street, and it was a battle to get aboard the train, standing room only. Thousands travelled this way. When many families arrived in Southend they went straight to the shop, or house, hiring out babies prams, which saved the parents the job of carrying the offspring about. Some went for the trip on the pier train, or the sailing boats, such as the 'Skylark', or a trip in the Kursaal, for all the fun of the fair. The same conditions prevailed to get home by train, but they never went home without rocks and cockles.

During the years when we were all children of the one family, we all found our own pursuits and friends. The brothers' tastes differed from the sisters'. On holiday time there was always a fair on Blackheath, and on one occasion we decided to go with some friends to Blackheath. Mum made us up some food, and we gathered in some spending money. We started off with the house dog at our heels, which Mum had asked us to take to give it a run. To get to our destination we had to walk along the old Brunswick Road, and across East India Dock Road, to Blackwall Tunnel. There was no means of transport through there, and we had to walk along the narrow pavement which ran through the tunnel for pedestrians. When we walked out the other end, we had to go up Tunnel Avenue, cross the road, and then climb up Vanbrugh Hill, which was very steep, and on to Blackheath. Here was all the fun of the fair, coconut shies and so on. We tramped around there, and suddenly someone said 'Where's the dog?' We searched, but could not find it. We went home a different way, walking off the Heath into Greenwich Park, examined the chart of 'Greenwich Mean Time', the 'Meridian Line', also the Observatory. We walked through the Park, and then down King William Street, by the College and Hospital, and the pier where the steamers used to call, on the way down the river to Southend and Margate. We walked under the river via the subway, which had a lift at each end. At the other end we were in Cubitt Town, and walked home through Millwall, and over the Dock Bridges, and Prestons Road, through Cotton Street and down Brunswick Road, on the way to where we lived, in Andrew Street. We never won anything at the Blackheath Fair, and having devoured our lunch, we were tired and hungry. When we got to the street door, the dog was sitting there.

Blackwall Tunnel was not very wide and only horse traffic used it. Boys used to be employed there, clearing up the dung. They dodged in and out of the horses hoofs, and it was amazing how they kept the confines and roads of the tunnel so clean. Another of our childhood trips was to walk through Chrisp Street up Guildford Road, to 'Stink House Bridge', and along Bow Common to Burdett Road, and Grove Road, thence on to Victoria Park. One section of the park had a boating lake, and all sorts of sports. It contained a swimming lake, and we undressed on the promenade surrounding it. We had our swim, dressed, and walked home again. We had to pass a shop at the bottom of Chrisp Street, where the window was filled with steaming hot fruit puddings on sale, and round the corner, by the 'Wooden Bridge', was a toffee making shop. These combined smells gave us a great appetite, after our outing. Another trip was to walk over the Iron Bridge to Canning Town, and turn into Victoria Dock Road, keep right on through Tidal Basin and Silvertown, to North Woolwich, where we boarded the Woolwich Free Ferry. When on the other side we went through Beresford Square and up to Plumstead Common, where the barracks were. We went to see the Church Parade which was performed the first Sunday in the month. The march past, behind the Military Bands, was an inspiring sight. This walk took us past where the 'HMS Thunderer' was built and launched, also the Royal Group of Docks. There was no limit to what one could do in those young days, when health and vitality abounded.

4.

Entertainment

I remember the two music halls in Poplar. One was 'The Queen's' in High Street Poplar near Robin Hood Lane. The street outside was very narrow, and the patrons used to queue up in the middle of the road, as there was no traffic passing up and down in those days. It was run by a family who had been the owners for many years. It was opened in the eighteen hundreds and was demolished in the fifties during the rebuilding of Poplar. The other was the Poplar 'Hippodrome' which was also opened in the eighteen hundreds, and was originally known as the 'Princes'. It was on the Gulliver Hippodrome Circuit. After many years, as a music hall, it was converted into a cinema. It was demolished in the fifties, and a housing estate was erected on the site, named after George Lansbury. It was situated at the corner of Stainsby Road in East India Dock Road.

Just before the first great war, it was the usual thing to have one night a week out at a performance at the 'Queen's'. There were four entrances: the Gallery, the Balcony, the Pit and the Stalls. The Pit and Gallery queue extended right down to Cotton Street. The Balcony and the Stalls were in the opposite direction. There was a system of 'early doors' which was extra to the normal charge. This allowed the patrons the pick of the seats before the main lot went in. Whilst the crowd were waiting for the signal to enter, they were regaled by the efforts of the buskers, giving of their best in fair weather or foul, before taking the hat round to gather in the coppers. There were dancing acts, cornet playing, male and female songsters, the barrel organ playing ditties of the time, glass eaters, and chain escapologists. They had to work fast, fighting against time, before the traps were sprung and the crowd began to file in the various entrances. The Tuppenny Rush or Gallery Section made a mad rush, everyone for themselves, passing over the two-penny admission fee (this was old currency), drawing their tickets and making a mad rush up the stairs to the top of the building. These stairs were illuminated by gas jets in wire frames. A rush was made inside. After giving the ticket up the first ones in clomped down the steps of the gallery to the front row, the favourite spot. They sat on the steps as there were no seats. Before settling down, those that had the wealth made their way to the back of the gallery for a cheesecake and a bottle of Idris Lemonade for refreshment.

Queens Theatre,
Poplar High Street,
1930
(Local History Library,
Tower Hamlets Libraries)

Poplar Hippodrome,
East India Dock Road,
1949 (built 1905)
(Local History Library,
Tower Hamlets Libraries)

Many of the regular patrons of the 'loft' or gallery, and students from local colleges and hospitals playfully threw peanut shells over the top on to some of the rich people in the stalls below. Suddenly the lights would go up to signal the commencement of the performance. The orchestra filed into the orchestra pit – all six of them. The pianist knew everyone who passed him, and he always had a smile. In came the violinist, the trombonist, the trumpeter, and the drummer, and finally on to the dais came Morris, the conductor. He was an outstanding violinist, and was a master of all types of music. When the orchestra struck up the 'William Tell' overture, the drummer came into his own, rendering the terrific rolls on the drums.

There was a long bar running from the stage to the middle of the pit with a long brass rail, waist high. All the elite, after collecting their drinks at the bar, used to walk over and lean on the rail, watching the stage show. In the bar hung a large painting of Charles Austin the comedian, and the barmaid never altered her smart appearance all the years I went there for the entertainment.

On either side of the stage was a frame. These were used by two page boys, who inserted the number of the act coming on, and also whether 'extra turn' or 'deputy' or 'intermission'. These were later substituted by electric lettering. The heavy safety curtain had to be lowered at every performance in case of fire. An appeal was made on all programmes, asking that patrons would remove any headgear likely to interfere with the view of anyone seated behind. There were two performances at night, the first house and the second house, and sometimes a matinee in the afternoon. Every show had a packed audience, from the 'gods' up in the attic, or gallery, to the stalls and pit. Of course, the stalls patrons would delicately clap their hands at a good performance, but the laddies up the top whistled or catcalled or hollered 'More More'.

The 'Queen's' music hall catered for all tastes. All types of variety appeared, also playlets, and full length plays. Some of the acts I repeatedly saw over the years, from 1910 onwards.

After school hours, I used to get a few bob doing various little jobs. I used to go to Thomas & Co. Tailors in Andrew Street to help with their measuring. I ran errands for a Mrs Millroy, a lady attached to her son's confectionery business, who also gave me a few hours a week washing labels off confectionery cans. I was also a lather boy in Mr Will Roger's Barber Shop.

Hence I was able to visit the two music halls on many occasions. Here are some of the acts I remember at the Queen's: G.H. Elliot – the singer of coon songs his face all blacked, and immaculate in frock coat and top hat sang 'Lily Of Laguna' and other favourites were followed by a soft shoe shuffle dance. Talbot O'Farrell, with his favourite Irish songs, sung with great feeling and clarity. He never needed a microphone, his voice reached the farthest corner of the house. There was Wilkie Bard – star comedian. Tucker – the Singing Violinist with his £1000 Strad. He sang and fiddled straight and syncopated music. Billy Russell, the 'Working Man' addressing the crowd. Harry Weldon 'It's no use', George Formby senior attired in a long coat, down to his ankles, stood rigid in the middle of the stage, handing out his jokes, and a rendering of 'I was standing on the Corner of the Street'. He never took the blank look off his face, even when he nodded to acknowledge the applause of the audience. Also George Formby Junior, with his guitar, patter and songs like 'Chinese Laundry Blues'. George Carney 'The Fool of the Force' patter, and 'Major General Worthington' song, completed the act. Issy Bonn with his Jewish jokes sang songs with great gusto and powerful voice. In the very early days of the new form of transport, the automobile, Harry Tate with his large whiskers gave a motoring sketch. Harry Champion, with his Cockney dress, sang songs – all at quick fire timing, finishing with a little step dance, to the tune of 'Any Old Iron'. Jack Pleasant's the 'Lancashire Lad' complete with buttonhole flower and simple patter made us laugh. George Jackley, and in later years, Nat Jackley, the guardsman dance, complete with busby, had to be seen to be believed. Great pantomime artists, they both were. There were, of course, many others, whom I never saw but who remain in the memories of many of the older folk. I can remember, when a revue was presented at the Queen's, and although it must have been around 1920 when I saw it, I cannot forget the first appearance of the fabulous Gracie Fields from Lancashire. Her range of voice, when singing, was perfect, and anyone could see she was destined for stardom, and she soon rose from the 'Mr Tower of London' revue at the East End Queen's Music Hall, to world wide fame. I can also remember Gertie Gitana, who sang beautiful songs, such as 'Nellie Dean', also Betty Driver, who often used to 'step in' for Gracie Fields, when she couldn't appear. Who can forget the fun of Nellie Wallace, with her comedy and her funny songs and make up, Hylda Baker, in her own brand of antics, and of course the favourite Cockney Commediene Kate Carney, the Pearly Queen of the East End. One of the plays performed at the Queen's was 'Humanity' starring John Lawson. He used to advertise outside the theatre on hoardings 'China purchased at a fabulous price, broken at every performance'. The final scene was set in a drawing room, and finishing touches were provided by a fire, and a fight throwing china about. The show finished with John Lawson on his knees singing 'Only a Jew'. Tod Slaughter starred in 'The Demon Barber of Fleet Street'. He ushered his customers into a chair, which stood on a trap door in the floor. When the time was ripe, he pulled a hidden lever, and the unfortunate occupant of the barber's chair was thrown into a pit below. Later he did a good trade with pies, supposedly made from the victims. In 'Dick Turpin Highwayman' they had a horse, on the stage, to portray Dick Turpin's famous horse character. When the play came to the end, the finale was provided by the highwayman shouting to the animal as he mounted, 'Away, away, Bonny Black Bess, to York!' It crossed the stage and dashed through the open french windows. This provoked loud cheers and claps from everyone. At various times full length plays were performed, such as some I witnessed, 'Uncle Tom's Cabin', 'Why Girls Leave Home', 'The Red Barn', and 'The Fighting Parson'. The waxed moustached villain in the shows had to be full of dirty tricks, capable of fetching on the tears of the women, and catcalls calling him wicked names. He had to be smuggled out of a back entrance for his own safety.

The Poplar Hippodrome was a music hall depicting variety acts and small playlets of drama or comedy. In the early days, when I went there, I saw many great acts, due mainly to the fact that the music hall was on the Gulliver Circuit, which ran the Hippodromes in various areas, and also West End Halls, thus being able to attract all the best talent in show business. I have seen and enjoyed some of the following artists dating back to 1909, when I first went to music halls. Little Tich with his big Boots, Tommy Trinder, Max Wall, Frank Randel, George Robey (the Prime Minister of Mirth). He was attired in a frock coat and narrow bowler hat. His eyebrows were thickly painted and he stood in the middle of the stage doing his act. Two of his items were: 'Your intellectual powers are not sufficiently developed to comprehend the veracity of my statement', 'You are slightly intoxicated with the exuberance of your own verbosity'. G.H. Chirgwin 'The White Eyed Kaffir'. His most famous songs were 'A Poor Blind Boy', which used to 'bring the house down', and 'My Fiddle is My Sweetheart', unforgettable pathos. Charles Coburn with his famous song 'The Man who Broke the Bank at Monte Carlo'. Max Miller who bounded on to the stage to the strains of his signature tune 'Mary Mary from the Dairy'. He walked to the footlights with his tuxedo hat at a jaunty angle, looked to the wings; left and right, as though he didn't want the stage manager to hear. 'Which book do you want, the good, or bad?' and so he went on, putting over 'double meaning' jokes at top speed. The audience loved it and he always remained top of the bill. Among the female artists I remember in the nineteen hundreds were Daisy Dormer, Maidie Scott, Florrie Forde, Ella Shields (Male Impersonator), Ida Barr and the escapologist Houdini. No chains or trussing up, under any adverse conditions, such as water, heights, enclosed cases, could prevent him escaping in record time. The Great Carmo, Horace Goldin, Chung Ling Soo, illusionists, (the latter died on the stage through an accident in one of his tricks), Doctor Bodie an electrical magician, ventriloquists Clarkson Rose, Arthur Prince and Coram, around 1912 were all great favourites.

These two music halls always had a pantomime at Christmas time, and the atmosphere inside the music hall was always festive. There was a great smell of oranges, nuts and cakes, and ginger beer, together with the cigarette smoke, and cheroots. The kids chatter and laughter and shouts were enjoyed by their parents as much as the show. Bank Holidays and Christmas time, made the Music Hall the mecca of old and young alike. If a change was desired, there was, within distance, the Imperial Palace at Canning Town, the Paragon at Mile End, Bow Palace at Bow, East Ham Palace at East Ham, and Stratford Empire, Theatre Royal, Borough Theatre at Stratford. I can remember, on Bank Holidays, the proprietors used to have flags and pennants hanging outside the 'Queen's', from 'Pewseys' in Robin Hood Lane and 'The Ship' in High Street Poplar pubs, past the gallery entrance. A favourite act, at the time was then something new in the entertainment world. It was a posing act, performed by an artiste who was billed as 'La Milo'. The rule at that time was, no movement was allowed. The lads visited the Music Hall in large numbers and the tale had gone round that 'All she wore was a Smile'. An announcer appeared in front of a drop curtain and explained her pose, such as 'Love Locked Out', 'September Morn', etc. The days of variety gradually lost favour with the patrons, and the Revue became more popular. Usually it had a chorus of dancing girls and a good comedian and the show was built around him. A singer and skits of comedy completed the show.

Round about 1908 there appeared something new in the field of entertainment. This was during our childhood days, when after school hours the streets were poorly lit. Fogs were everywhere in the winter months, and naturally the youngsters, and their parents, were eagerly seeking anything that would brighten up their outlook in the drab surroundings of those days. On the scene, then, came a wonderful idea. The Reverend Tyldesley, the pastor at the Poplar and Bromley Tabernacle, in Brunswick Road, commenced showing pictures on Thursday evenings in the Chapel. These were Magic Lantern with still slides, or a very early model of a cinematograph show. Children were admitted to the first performance, and parents the second. A large sheet was hung on the rostrum, which could be pulled up and down, before and after the show. There was a gallery, running the length of the hall, and at the far end of the gallery, a projection box had been erected, which housed the cinematograph. During the summer months, the Reverend Gentleman had curtains installed in the windows, so that light could not penetrate, to spoil the view of the films. He always gave a speech before the show commenced, and went to great lengths to impress the children, of the tremendous expense that had been entailed to enable this to be done, so that they would still have their entertainment in the summer. He asked us not to kick the backs of the seats in front, in excitement at the adventures of Lt Rose, one of the prevailing heroes of the time. Their few coppers of admission would not allow for payments of any damage. For us children the excitement was intense and we were glad when the introductory prayers had been completed. For many years the Music Halls and Theatres enjoyed the popularity of the public with no opposition, but suddenly a rival entertainment appeared on the horizon. I refer to the silent films appearing at 'Picture Palaces'. Some had a white sheet, suspended tightly, over which water was squirted before the show commenced, or even a white painted wall. The seating consisted of forms, and flooring all concrete. The first Picture Palace I remember was the 'Empire' in East India Dock Road, opposite Woolmore Street. Then there was 'The Star' in High Street Poplar. It was a case of lining up outside, where the attendant on duty was periodically shouting out at the top of his voice, 'Standing only in the ha'pennies'. This form of entertainment was springing up everywhere such as 'Grand Palace', 'Poplar Pavilion', 'The Gaiety', all in East India Dock Road, and the interior decorations were improving rapidly. Better screens, improved fireproofed projection boxes, spring-backed covered seats, lady ushers with hand torch, to guide you to your seat, piano accompaniment to the silent film. Usually there were two feature films, and a News Reel and the performance was continuous. Chocolates and ices were sold by attendants from trays on wheels. The pianist had to operate in a curtained off enclosure. The music had to be adapted to the theme of the film, such as exciting, or sad and tearful passages, and the timing was important. As time went on, a violin was added, even a cello. In some of the sad moments of a film the musicians must have been crying their eyes out and too upset to eat or drink their lunch, during a break. The silent films reigned for years, running in opposition to the theatre and Music Halls. Characters emerged on to the scene and became household names. Some of these early films are shown even today, such as Laurel and Hardy, and Charles Chaplin, and they are as popular as they were all those years ago. All tastes had to be catered for, some liked a good laugh, others a good 'western' or adventure, and, of course, the ladies liked to have a handkerchief at the ready and enjoy a good 'weepie'.

The Picture Palaces were assuming the title of Cinemas, and new luxurious ones were appearing such as the Troxy in Commercial Road. It had a well carpeted auditorium, with circle above, a large stage, and an electric organ operated by the organist Bobby Pagan. There was also an orchestra which accompanied appearing artists who performed between films. There was a very small old cinema a few doors away, which might have been in danger of closing, with the opposition of the new cinema, but the proprietors of the new cinema, kept it open, for the sake of sentiment – it was their mother who ran it. Then came another blow to the music halls and theatres. It was the 'talking' film, and it took the town by storm. People couldn't believe that the characters on the film would be speaking out from the screen, and they all had to flock to the 'cinemas' to see this wonderful discovery.

General Strike May 1926. Troops marching along East India Dock Road to the Docks
(Local History Library, Tower Hamlets Libraries)

5.

Politics

Poplar, throughout the years, has witnessed many scenes of strife, from the start of the century. It has always been a working class area, and in later years always elected a Labour candidate to the local council, and to the House of Commons, as a Member of Parliament. A great number of the workers were members of a trade union, so that their interests could be dealt with between elected officers, and the representatives of industrial concerns. Years ago a certain degree of secrecy had to be maintained, and weekly union meetings of the members were often held in the upstairs room of a public house. Before the meeting commenced, a doorkeeper was appointed to be at the door, which had a small pigeon hole inserted. He had to examine any entrant to the room, before entry. Usually, every member was known to him by sight, but he had to hold office during the period of branch meeting, and was voted to the post accordingly.

It was not always a Labour man, elected as a representative of the people, and years ago in Poplar the main candidate was a Liberal. When an election was in full swing, children used to parade the streets, for the fun of it, and this was one of the songs:

Vote vote for Sidney Buxton
Punch old Borthwick in the eye
If it wasn't for the Law
We would punch him in the jaw
And he wouldn't come voting anymore

Sir Alfred Yeo was a stalwart of the Liberal Party. He had a very smart appearance, and was a well known and popular figure, always standing outside his shop in St Leonards Road Poplar. He always gave everyone a cheery smile. Poplar Town Hall, situated in Newby Place opposite Poplar Church has been the scene of much activity throughout the years. It has been the scene of political meetings, Trade Union gatherings, Poplar Borough Council meetings, entertainments and all manner of civic gatherings. Many famous people have appeared on its stage, political leaders, Members of the Borough Council, Trade Union leaders, from all branches of the Movement.

Among them were J.H. Thomas, Will Crooks, Will Thorne, Ben Tillet, George Lansbury, John Scurr, J.R. Clynes, Clement Attlee, Emmanuel Shinwell, Herbert Morrison and Ramsey McDonald.

I remember the 1926 strike, when industry was forced to a halt, and all the unions were involved in support of the miners. There were many scenes of violence, and I can recall when there were many lorries lined up in East India Dock Road and alongside East India Dock Walls all immobilised. Troops were marching down the road, even small tanks were brought in and any sign of hanging about in bunches was immediately dealt with by moving on the offenders. It went on for some time, and eventually there were mass meetings, and after advice by the leaders it was called off. It received the name of 'Black Friday', and a large number of workers were a long time getting back to work. Only essential labour was employed until things had begun to straighten out again in trading etc. Only relief assistance available was help for wife and children, some of the husbands, which included my father and brother in law, were sent to Hallesley Bay, or Dunton Farm Colony, for special training to fit them for other work. During the 1926 strike there were meetings with leaders from the miners – dockers – railwaymen – electricians – transport workers – and representatives of all types of labour, and always, when proceedings had finished, the Chairman asked for a vote of thanks, and the whole audience stood up, and with great gusto roared out the strains of 'The Red Flag'.

The old Poplar Council Offices, in High Street Poplar, are still there, although not used for the general council work, as before. There were trees along Brunswick Road, Poplar, but that was not enough for George Lansbury, who had trees planted all round the Borough to make a more cheerful atmosphere for everyone. He followed up by installing the 'Lido' in Hyde Park. George Lansbury used to travel on the District underground line to Westminster from Bow to carry out his duties as an M.P. in the House of Commons. He was always reading the morning news in the Daily Herald, but he was always ready for a chat should you approach him. His wonderful work for the poorer people of Poplar will never be forgotten, and indeed, a new housing estate has been named in his honour.

George Green has a statue erected in his honour outside the Poplar Baths to honour him for the works he did for Poplar. It was considered a great achievement to qualify for admission to George Green's school in East India Dock Road. The Dock Gates enclosing the East India Dock, were the scene for religious meetings of the churches and Salvation Army who both had their bands playing there. All types of meetings were held there, and crowds used to gather and listen to the speeches. Demonstrations with banners flying used to form up there, and march through the East End and City and West End, to Hyde Park, and Tower Hill. Victoria Park was also a famous meeting place for any gatherings, which was reached by marching through Burdett Road and Grove Road, the Irish Pipe Bands used to furnish the marching tunes. There was the famous march, when George Lansbury and the Poplar Councillors marched with banners flying and to the strains of a band to undergo a prison sentence over levying of the Rates.

6.

Transport

In the early years of the century the Blackwall to Fenchurch Street line of the Great Eastern Railway had a station on the Blackwall Pier, and on in Brunswick Road, Poplar. Millwall Junction station, on the previous Great Eastern Railway system, served the Blackwall and Fenchurch Street Line. The station was reached by a footbridge, which extended from Harrow Lane off of High Street Poplar. This small train consisted of a locomotive, and about three coaches and the stations in its passage were Millwall Junction, South Dock, Millwall, and North Greenwich, situated at Millwall, adjacent to Island Gardens. Greenwich itself was reached by a foot tunnel under the Thames. Poplar, also, was served by a station, in East India Dock Road, which was operated by the North London Railway, and South Bromley Station was in the Poplar area also. The line ran through Bow, Old Ford, Homerton, Hackney, Dalston Junction, Haggerston, and on to Broad Street.

The London County Council of those days ran a wonderful tram service, with very cheap fares, for the workers, who had to get to work early. The horse drawn trams used to start, and finish, at Blackwall Tunnel, and when the horse were changed there, they used to be released from the tram, and walk to the stables, in Aberfeldy Street. As time went on, trolleys were used, and the tramway system was electrified. The trams were made more weatherproof, especially for the driver, who used to have to operate the controls, exposed to the weather, and so the passengers and staff operating the trams, were able to travel in comfort with the minimum exposure to weather conditions. The tram fare, at the Workman Rate Return was 2d between Blackwall Tunnel and Aldgate, and from Blackwall Tunnel to Bloomsbury it was 4d Return or Blackwall Tunnel to Barking Broadway – the same fourpence Return. This was, of course, after the tram service was extended from Poplar to Barking. The tram service went on until 1952.

The bus services extended to more distant thoroughfares, and there were no cheaper fares, such as the Workman's Return Ticket. The buses used to have open front, and were not very comfortable for the exposed driver and conductor. The top deck of the bus was reached by outside steps, exposed to the elements, and on the top, wooden seats were in use, and on the back of

Old Poplar Town Hall, Newby Place – from a photo 1871
(Local History Library, Tower Hamlets Libraries)

Poplar Station 1927 (Local History Library, Tower Hamlets Libraries)

the seat, in front of where anyone was sitting, was a tarpaulin sheet, to place over knees, when the weather was inclement.

If it was cold, you had to stand it, but people got used to it. What a difference today it is, with crew and passengers under cover, and comfortable cushioned seats. Years ago, there were no buses running to Millwall, and none through the Blackwall Tunnel, and people had to walk to their destinations. Both the tram and bus services provided a very valuable service to East End people, and both ran all night. The trams operated between Blackwall Tunnel and Bloomsbury both ways, and the buses from Charing Cross to Becontree Heath, likewise. These were very handy to early morning workers.

7.

World Wars

The misery and suffering of war took its toll on everyone. Shortness of food, which meant rationing of what we had, the blackout, the curtailment of all forms of everyday life, the worry of every family, concerning relatives, whether at home, or miles away, in different climes. The battlefields took their toll of lives and injuries, and the battles for survival were bitter. In the First World War, the air bombardments were not so severe as the second one, mainly by a few 'Fokker' or 'Tanbe' aeroplane raids, augmented also by the Zeppelin airships, who raided at night. The 'Harry' public house in Brunswick Road, Poplar, received a bomb, and also the children suffered death and injury when their school, in North Street Poplar, was hit from the air by a bomb. A memorial to this exists in the entrance to the Recreation Ground Park in East India Dock Road, Poplar.

The air war was a different proposition in the Second World War, causing great damage to life and property. Massed air raids were the order of the day, and it went on by day and night. Poplar was in the midst of a dock area, and was a constant target for attacking aircraft. Rows of houses, shops, factories, roads, churches, in fact everything was vulnerable. Many of us had friends or relatives killed or wounded, and everyone suffered from the effects of fire and blast. Every morning wer had to get out early to work, by the best means we could. We were working all day in London, and up all night as Wardens, or members of decontamination squads, ambulance men, relief fire men, helping to put incendiaries out, or dig out anyone trapped, and trying to clear up any mess in one's own house, damaged by 'blast'. Very little sleep was had, and any grub had to be got when you could get it. Heavy bombers, buzz bombs and rockets came over, and the tethered balloons probably kept them up higher in the sky.

The schools were opened midday for meals, provided at a cheap rate, which were a boon to husbands working in the area and whose wives and children had been evacuated to safer areas in the country. Those that were in the Capital, had to sleep in Anderson shelters, indoor shelters, church vaults, underground basements, or the tube stations. Some of the railways in the area, which had warehouse accommodation, used to open up the basements,

George Lansbury and Poplar councillors march to the High Court during Poplar Rates Dispute, 1921

(Local History Library, Tower Hamlets Libraries)

and some laid on First Aid personnel and Fire Volunteers. A wonderful spirit of comradeship was built up, and the people taking shelter were regaled with concerts and sing songs to keep the atmosphere cheerful. East India Dock Road, and the area all around was filled with South Africans, Indians, Canadians, Australians, and New Zealanders and the 'Dough Boys' from America, always at the ready when asked 'Got any Gum Chum?' Many of them married Poplar girls, who went back with them to America, when the war finished. Every colour and religion was present here in Poplar, during those fateful days, and their presence here cheered everyone up in the hour of need. Poplar was severely damaged, and all its buildings were knocked to ruins, and the population split up. Out of all the ruin, and carnage, rose all the modern tower blocks. Whole streets were wiped out in the process of rebuilding, to make way for new roads and living accommodation, and it seems that a new population has taken over, and the old one has transferred to different territory. When the houses were blown down, or pulled down, by the bulldozer, it seemed that the old world of landscapes and neighbours had disappeared. A new environment had appeared, different buildings, and friendships, and new ways of life had become apparent. Is it possible that the old Poplar atmosphere of good neighbourliness will be sustained by the new?

8.

Moving Out

From about the year 1926, the London County Council, under the chairmanship of Herbert Morrison, embarked on schemes to try to alleviate the terrible housing shortage in the London areas under their jurisdiction. East and West, North and South, wherever land was available on the outskirts of London, they planned, and started building new estates, so that the victims of overcrowding could be accommodated in more comfortable homes, open surroundings. The cottages they built had a front and back garden, two bedrooms, living room, scullery and bathroom, and indoor toilet. The rent was fourteen shillings and fivepence weekly. Many of the Poplar and East End people took this opportunity of rehousing, especially on the new Becontree Estate, at Dagenham, which was turning a rural area into a vast housing estate. At first, there was only a small station at Dagenham, in the old village, and one at Dagenham Dock. There used to be a little hump back bridge, over the railway, no pavements, only a road wide enough for horse and cart. There used to be a stall on the bridge where one could purchase fish and chips. Vast changes have taken place throughout the years. The railway Authorities have built new stations, extending the 'underground' section to Upminster, shops have been opened, cinemas and ample facilities to get to neighbouring Barking, Romford and Ilford shopping centres. The foresight of those people years ago, who eased the problems of Poplar, regarding overcrowding, is remarkable. One can imagine what it would have been like today, without those plans being put into operation. The old original 'Iron Bridge', that used to divide Poplar from Canning Town, over Bow Creek Waterway, had a plate in the middle of it, which had an inscription on it stating that half the bridge was in Essex, and the other Middlesex. Anyone living in the Middlesex zone was eligible for rehousing by the London County Council.

Proper accommodation was hard to obtain around the Poplar area, and when I was first married, like most other young people in their early years of marriage, I was glad to live at the wife's mother's place, in very limited accommodation, and when a child arrived, the wife and I had to explore any avenues that were available, to get better facilities, to fetch up our child. We decided to approach the housing authority of the council, to have our names included on the list. We were eventually successful in our application, and were allocated a two bedroomed cottage at Dagenham. When we moved, it meant the breaking of all our ties, with both our families, and the neighbours of many years, and we could only hope that it would be for the best in surroundings that were so different to what we had always been brought up in. I had to leave home very early in the morning, and travel to my work on the railway at Poplar from the little country station at Dagenham, and was away from home all day. When I got home at night, the wife was miserable, not being used to the new surroundings and strange people, and so we had to admit that notwithstanding the comfort of the new cottage and the general atmosphere, it somehow didn't suit us, and so after a few months I managed to get a flat in Grosvenor Buildings, at Poplar and we moved back. We had several addresses in Poplar, but towards the end of the Second War, owing to blast damage, we again returned to Dagenham, which was vastly different to the early days.

When I was a boy Poplar was a thriving place. There were a hundred or more shops in St Leonards Road, and a like amount in the old Chrisp Street Market. Nearly all of those shops, which played such a vital part in the life of old Poplar, have gone, and what a sad thing it was, that the old friendship which existed between shopkeeper and customer, has been swept away. Nearly all the old pubs have gone, where the older population of Poplar spent so many convivial hours with a cheap glass of beer, and enjoyed the company of the 'regulars'. The old cinemas, The Grand Palace, Poplar Pavilion, The Gaiety, The Empire, The Star, have all closed. The only two music halls, The Poplar Hippodrome and the Queens have disappeared. What memories the old people have of these places. The Poplar Hospital, after years of healing, is closed, the nurses in Bow Lane have gone. The Churches of St Frideswides, St Michael and All Angels, St Saviours Bromley, St Leonards have gone, or shut down, and all services are now held in St Matthias and Poplar Church. The North London Railway, and all the goods and freight depots operating in the Poplar area, which once had connections to any part of England, have gone. Whole rows of houses, and streets have gone to give place to modern planning. Many industries have moved away to other areas, and so have many people who lived and worked in old Poplar.

Millwall and Blackwall lie on the banks of the River Thames, the gateway to the oceans of the world. Surely, in the East End, there are all the facilities that industry needs? The most vital needs are for road, rail and river assets, and a large labour force. What a wonderful thing it would be if the Council could join forces with British and foreign industrialists to re-develop the area, and make Poplar Docks and Millwall again the hive of industry it was once.

John Blake was born in Poplar at the turn of the century and began work on the railways in the East End in 1913, remaining in the same job for over fifty years. Mr Blake died in 1984.